CRANWELL
RNAS & RAF PHOTOGRAPHS

Midland Publishing
Limited

© 1993
Peter H T Green and Mike Hodgson
and
Midland Publishing Limited

Published by
Midland Publishing Limited
24 The Hollow, Earl Shilton
Leicester, LE9 7NA
England

ISBN 0-85780-014-1

Printed in England by
The Nuffield Press Limited
Cowley, Oxford
OX9 1TR

Designed by
Midland Publishing
and Stephen Thompson Associates

Front cover illustration: **Four Cranwell-based de Havilland Vampire FB.9s, WX221, WX225, WX215 and WR264 – coded 4, 8, 12 and 29 respectively, formate over the College Hall in mid-1957. The FB.9s provided single-seat end-on training to the Provost/Vampire T.11 syllabus of the day.** Flight 34974s.

Title page illustration: **Often called the Lynx-Avro, the Avro 504N was designed as a replacement for the ageing 504K, an aeroplane with its roots firmly in the Great War. Production commenced in 1925 and almost 600 aircraft were built before it ended in 1932. The 'N' began to appear at Cranwell in 1927** and remained on strength until replaced by the Avro Tutor in 1933. The aircraft in this 1932 A Flight line-up are – K1820/1, J750/2 (one of two prototypes), J8507/3, K1052/4, J8548/5, K1808/6, K1251/7 and F8713/8 (the latter being a converted '504K). The significance of the dark fuselage panels is unknown.

CRANWELL

ROYAL NAVAL AIR SERVICE & ROYAL AIR FORCE PHOTOGRAPHS

Peter Green and Mike Hodgson

INTRODUCTION

The beginnings of flying at Cranwell go back to mid-1915 when the Royal Navy was looking for a training airfield. The open spaces of the heathland south of Lincoln were suitable and the Admiralty, under the Defence of the Realm Act, took charge of just over 3000 acres of farmland to the west of Cranwell village on 23rd November 1915.

It was decided that facilities should be available for training officers and men on Balloons and Airships as well as aeroplanes. By mid-December 1915, and in gloomy wet weather, the first personnel were arriving, the officers taking possession of the farmhouse and other ranks taking over the farm cottages and barn.

The story of RNAS Cranwell/HMS *Daedalus* and Royal Air Force Cranwell follows in pictures. The majority of these have come from the library at Cranwell and we are indebted to the College Librarian and Archivist, Mrs Jean M Buckberry ALA, for access to these and the permission of the Commandant to use them. All photographs are from this source unless otherwise credited. Others come from various sources and these are credited to the immediate supplier unless the original source is known, because in many cases it is now impossible to determine the actual photographer. If any are not properly credited, we apologise. We are grateful for the help we have received.

Needless to say, any additional photographs would be very welcome on loan for copying and return. In particular, the authors would welcome illustrations covering the period of the Second World War, 1939-45. It is hoped to produce a second volume in due course.

Peter Green
Mike Hodgson   September 1993

FIRST ARRIVALS

Above: Naval ratings help to clear the last of the farm produce from a site that was soon to become a bustling flying station. The stone walls, typical of the area, were also to disappear – to be used to make hard roads from the existing cart tracks to enable the constructor's vehicles to reach the site. The photograph is dated December 1915.

Right: Most probably built in the late eighteenth century as a gamekeeper's cottage, The Lodge, which by 1914 was a farm house, was requisitioned for use as the Commodore's residence. During the Great War it was doubled in size by adding an eastern half; the design and construction matching that of the original building. Apart from the period 1939-1945, when it was used as an officers' mess for both RAF and WRAF officers attending courses at Cranwell, the Lodge has been used as the Commandant's residence. It is seen here in December 1915.

Above: A Chief Petty Officer with thirty five men arrived at Cranwell from Eastchurch and the Isle of Grain on 16th December 1915 to begin work on the new training establishment for the Royal Naval Air Service. Almost all of the group are seen here in December 1915, in front of the gardener's cottage to Lodge Farm, requisitioned as billets for this founding force.

Photograph on the opposite page: This undated photograph shows B.E.2c No.1738 undergoing servicing in one of the Cranwell hangars.

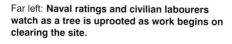

Far left: Naval ratings and civilian labourers watch as a tree is uprooted as work begins on clearing the site.

Left: These vehicles – including a traction engine, the only form of heavy haulage available – photographed in front of the Lodge Farm labourers' cottages, were among the first vehicles to arrive on the site.

Centre Left: Construction work began on 28th December 1915 and work on the first huts proceeded apace. The wood and corrugated iron structures seen here, provided little comfort for the first Naval trainees to arrive when the station opened on 1st April 1916.

Below: Commodore Godfrey Paine, first Commandant of the RNAS Central Training Establishment, Cranwell, part of the strength of HMS Daedalus, **pictured with his staff officers in front of the original wood and corrugated iron headquarters building, in 1916.**

Right: **The first aeroplane to be delivered to Cranwell was B.E.2 No.3999 which made the journey from Chingford on 15th January 1916. The B.E. series, which had its origins in 1912, became the most widely used training aeroplane at Cranwell during the Great War. This is a typical example. No.3999 was reduced to instructional use on 8th May 1916.**

Below: **With construction forging ahead the camp begins to take shape. Taken in September 1916, this aerial view shows huts yet to receive roofs as well as bell tents still in use to house the workforce. The South airfield hangars are visible to the top right of the photograph. By the following May, squads of parading ratings had replaced the bell tents on the parade square and aeroplanes were operating from the South airfield. Soon afterwards the first pair of two-storey barrack blocks were erected just to the right of the white roofed building in the top left of this photograph. Also, a Bessonneau hangar, said to house a Maurice Farman biplane, was soon to occupy the open area in the top left of this photograph. A site plan, as at 1918, is featured on page 12.**

Above: **Avro 504A No.2930 after a landing accident. The aeroplane has perhaps been involved in an earlier mishap since it sports the fin from a different machine (that of No.3307).** D S Glover

Below: **By May 1917 much of the initial building programme was complete. Squads of parading ratings have replaced the bell tents on the parade square and aeroplanes are operating from the South airfield. The three large** aeroplane sheds (D, E and F) in the top right of the photograph are believed to be F-types. Other buildings can be identified by referring to the site plan and key on pages 12 and 13.

Above: **The first Royal visit to Cranwell was made by HM King George V and Queen Mary on 20th July 1916. The King and Queen are seen here with their entourage walking across the yet to be completed North aerodrome.**

Above: **The contemporary caption to this photograph suggests that the Bessonneau hangar on the left of the picture was the first to be erected 'to house the Maurice Farman biplane'. However the construction of the two-storey barrack blocks indicates the photograph to have been taken after those on pages 7 and 8, neither of which feature the hangar. Perhaps the Bessonneau had been moved from another position on the station?**

Above: **An aerial view, from mid 1916, showing The Lodge, centre top, together with the nearby range of Victorian farm buildings. These buildings were commandeered by the first arrivals and are still in use as part of the Motor Transport yard. To the left of the picture is the first officers' mess building.**

Above: The first permanent hangars to be erected were situated on the North airfield. These and the other buildings can be identified from the site plan on page 12. On this photograph, dated 1st September 1916, we see The Lodge and original farm buildings in the upper right corner.

Left: **Construction of East Camp on the South airfield began late in 1917 and was well under way when this view was taken on 25th February 1918. These buildings, unlike the first timber and corrugated iron structures, were to be more permanent and were constructed in brick. The extensive railway system built to help construction is clearly seen. The special branch line was built to run from Sleaford to Cranwell to cater for workman's trains and for moving materials. It was extended to run across the North Airfield to reach the Lighter Than Air site and was used to move servicemen to and from Sleaford. It continued in use for passengers until 1927, but was not finally closed until August 1956**

Below left: **Sopwith Triplane N5351, the second production machine constructed by the Lincoln firm of Clayton and Shuttleworth, one of several Lincoln companies to build aeroplanes during the Great War, photographed on a visit to Cranwell in February 1917, prior to its delivery to 8 Squadron, RNAS, based at Vert Galand, France.**

Below right: **This aeroplane repair shop contains a large variety of aircraft, including DH.6, Avro 504 and Sopwith types awaiting repair or salvage. DH.9A E8534 is conspicuous in the foreground. This photograph is believed to have been taken in 1918.**

Above: **1919 postcard series photograph of the Motor Transport section. The buildings behind the vehicles are the original victorian farm buildings commandeered in 1915 – some of which are still in use today.**

Below left: **A 1918 interior view of the Gymnasium.**

Below: **The Railway Station at Cranwell, circa 1922.**

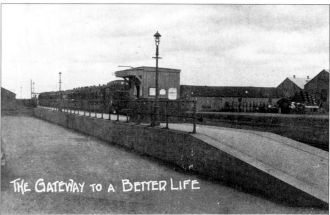

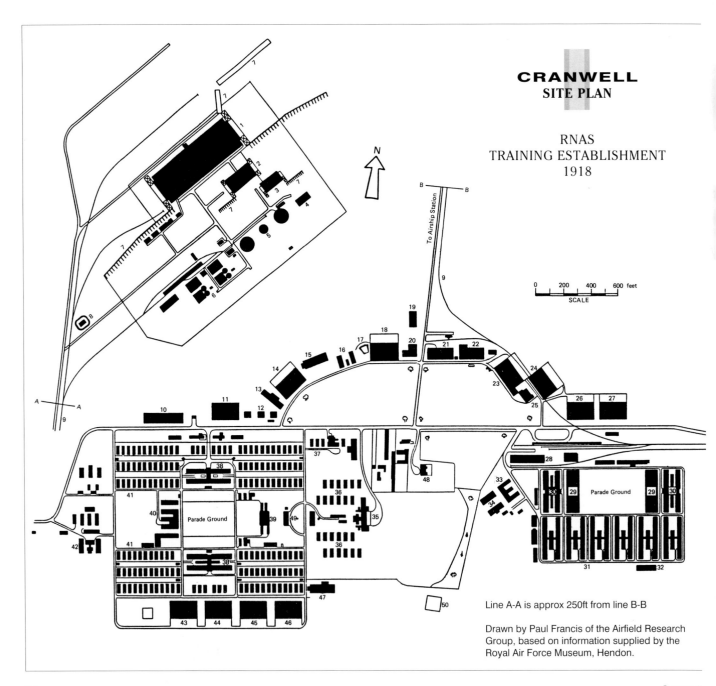

CRANWELL
SITE PLAN

RNAS
TRAINING ESTABLISHMENT
1918

Line A-A is approx 250ft from line B-B

Drawn by Paul Francis of the Airfield Research
Group, based on information supplied by the
Royal Air Force Museum, Hendon.

KEY TO SITE PLAN

1. Rigid airship shed No.1 (R) 700 x 150 x 100ft high
2. CP airship shed (Q) 220 x 70 x 70ft high
3. SS airship shed (shed P) 160ft x 45ft
4. Kite balloon hangar (removed)
5. Gas holders
6. Hydogen gas plant
7. Wind screen
8. Magazine
9. Camp railway
10. Engineers' shop
11. Store shed No.2
12. Water towers
13. Instructional lecture rooms
14. Instructional shop
15. Aeroplane shed N
16. Armament shop
17. Range
18. Aeroplane shed C
19. Test house
20. Power house
21. Aeroplane repair shop
22. Engine shop
23. Aeroplane repair shop
24. Store shed No.1
25. Dope and fabric shop
26. Aeroplane shed B
27. Aeroplane shed A
28. Technical store
29. Drill shed
30. Men's mess block
31. Men's dormitory blocks
32. Laundry
33. W/T block
34. Lecture rooms
35. Officers' mess
36. Officers' cabin blocks
37. Warrant officers' quarters
38. Men's mess
39. Drill shed
40. Canteen
41. Men's quarters
42. Sick quarters
43. Aeroplane shed G
44. Aeroplane shed F
45. Aeroplane shed E
46. Aeroplane shed D
47. Swimming baths and gymnasium
48. CO's house, Cranwell Lodge
49. Central offices (SMQ) with flagstaff
50. Compass swinging platform

Above: **The main entrance to East Camp. One of a series of photographic postcards produced towards the end of the Great War. On 1st April 1918 the Royal Naval Air Service and Royal Flying Corps were amalgamated to form the Royal Air Force. The profusion of** uniforms in this illustration points to a date soon after the new service was formed.

Below: **Another example from the postcard series, this time featuring the WRAF recreation room.**

LIGHTER THAN AIR

Below: **Balloon, kite balloon and airship flying was an important element of the Royal Naval Air Service during the Great War and the new station at Cranwell was earmarked as the centre for this training. The first hangar for the Lighter Than Air Section was erected in March 1916. It housed one kite balloon inflated, and a spare one, deflated. The first ascent was made on 4th April 1916 and by the end of that year ten officers had completed their training. The Wicker-basket from one of these balloons is visible on the right.**

Below right: **Interior detail of the Coastal airship shed. Note the padding attached to the wooden structure – in case of accidental contact by the airship.**

Left: **Building work on the large rigid shed of The Lighter Than Air Section can be seen in the centre foreground. Still in use on the site is the original canvas kite balloon hangar, featured above, top left. Construction of a portable Submarine Scout shed, brought in from Anglesey, is well advanced despite it having been damaged in a gale at the end of March 1916. This rigid shed was completed early in 1917; a second building was planned but was cancelled before construction started. Photograph dated 15th October 1916.**

14

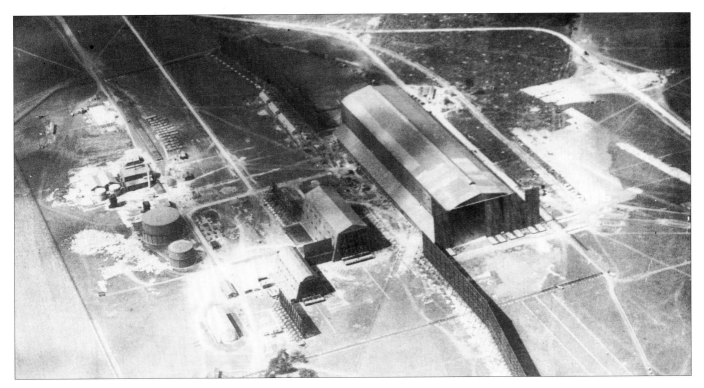

Above: **The completed Lighter Than Air Section
seen on 15th July 1917 looking westwards,
with, from the left, the kite balloon hangar, the
SS shed, coastal shed and large rigid shed.
The 90 ft high wind screens at each end of the
rigid shed enabled an airship to be 'walked
out' without fear of the craft being blown into
the shed and possibly being damaged.**

Right: **Aerial view of the Lighter Than Air
Section taken on the 4th September 1917. The
original canvas kite balloon shed had been
removed by this time. Both the North and
South aerodromes are clearly visible in this
view, looking south-west.**

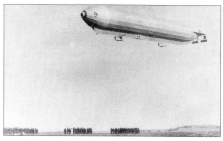

Above: **Rigid No.9 arrived at Cranwell on 15th October 1917 to give airship pilots some experience on rigid airships. Unfortunately she was compelled to land at Howden (Yorks) on 29th October and was damaged while being walked into the hangar there. She did not return to Cranwell, her place being taken by Rigid No.25.**

Above: **Submarine Scout airship with an American ground handling crew. Note the U.S. star marking on the fin. By 1918 the U.S. presence was slowly making itself felt after the United States entered the war in April 1917.**

Below: **Staff Officers of the Lighter Than Air Section photographed with American naval cadets who arrived at Cranwell in November 1917 to begin training as airship pilots.**

Above: **Under pressure from Air Marshal Trenchard, the Air Ministry decided in 1919 to establish a Royal Air Force College on the lines of Sandhurst and Dartmouth, for the purpose of training officers for permanent service. The College was inaugurated on 5th February 1920, when the first entry of 52 cadets arrived, 17 of them coming from the Royal Naval College at Dartmouth.**

Top left: **An unusual visiting aircraft was US Army Air Service DH4 AS6392? (last numeral obscured). Keen young cadets, identified by their white hat bands, inspect the cockpit.**

Above: **Cadets listen to a lecture in one of the bleak classrooms in the early days of the college.**

Left: **The hangars of the South airfield photographed in 1920, by now clearly marked for navigation purposes. Aircraft types include the Avro 504K.**

Top left: **The first Royal visit to the Royal Air Forces's new College took place a little over a month after it opened. Air Marshal Sir Hugh Trenchard, Chief of Air Staff, accompanied HRH The Prince Albert (later Duke of York and King George VI) on a visit to Cranwell and are seen here with Air Commodore C A H Longcroft, the College's first Commandant, and Wing Commander A L Godman, Assistant Commandant, taking the salute on 23rd March 1920.**

Centre top: **Old water towers, constructed in the early days of the station were demolished soon after the Great War. The German field gun in the right foreground is one of two such examples displayed in the old college gardens. One had been captured by Captain D H M Carbery (pilot) and Lt J B J Clements (observer) of 59 Squadron on 28th September 1918; the second was presented to GOC 11 Brigade RFC by General Plumer of the Second Army for services rendered against enemy batteries in the operations on the Messines Ridge on 7th June 1917.**

Top right: **Ready for inspection. A cadet's kit, laid out in regulation manner on his bed is ready for inspection. Note the heavy nailed boots.**

Above: **HRH Prince Albert and Air Commodore Longcroft inspect an Avro 504K, E3343, No.5 of C flight, 23rd March 1920. The aeroplane is unusual in that it has swastika symbols on the side and upper decking of the fuselage: the angle at which these have been applied suggest they are 'good luck' symbols.**

Above: **DH 9A H3557 of A Flight** sports a two colour fuselage band – could this be the initial use of the light blue/dark blue fuselage and wing marking that was to become standard to Cranwell aircraft in later years?

Right: **The Station Church.** The first church services were held in the gymnasium on the edge of the South airfield. Although still used for its original purposes during the week this was the first Church of St Michael and All Angels at Cranwell. When the College was founded it was necessary to find larger accommodation. A hangar on the North airfield was converted to become the church as seen in the photograph. Many aircraft parts became features of the church, the lights and altar fittings were made from propellers and the font incorporated aero-

engine cylinder heads supported by sections of propeller. Many items were transferred from the old hangar church when the new Church of St Michael and All Angels was dedicated on 1st June 1962.

Below: **B Flight on parade.** The Avro 504Ks of B Flight, together with both ground and air crews, line up for an unspecified parade in 1921.

Top: **Station Fire Service. A Crossley fire engine and crew – often needed with the many flying accidents of the early 'twenties. This photograph is dated 1921.**

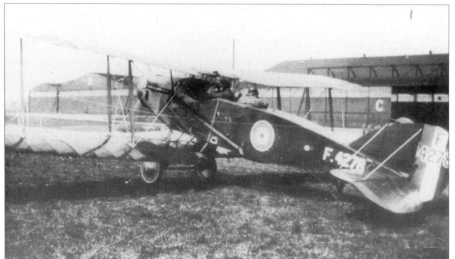

Left: **One of the three types to equip the College when it opened in 1920, the Bristol Fighter, or 'Brisfit' as it became known, was operated by B Flight. Over three thousand of the type had been built for the flying services during the Great War and production continued for the post war RAF, not ending until 1926. The peace-time air force used the Bristol Fighter for Army Co-operation duties and as a dual control trainer at Cranwell and with the University Air Squadrons. The Brisfit was superseded by the Armstrong Whitworth Atlas in 1930. F4278, pictured here, was the personal mount of the Commandant, Air Commodore Longcroft.**

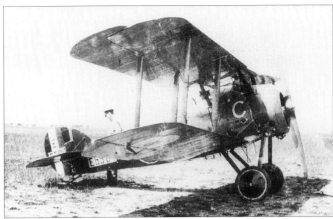

Top left: **Sopwith Snipes** were added to the flying school strength in 1921 when the original three flights were doubled to six. The Snipe had entered service with the RAF in September 1918 and due to the financial restrictions of the early post war years remained in squadron service until 1926 by which time it was the last rotary engined fighter to be operated. Snipes remained in service at flying schools a little longer and Cranwell's examples were phased out in 1927.

Above: **Instructor and pupil prepare for flight in a C Flight Avro 504K. Note the Gosport tube intercom system.**

Top right: **Sopwith Snipe E6501** arrived at Cranwell on 10th February 1922. Shortly afterwards, on a cross country flight, the pilot became lost in fog and in the ensuing forced landing at Harlington in Middlesex, the aircraft was stalled trying to miss a tree and wrecked as a result.

Lower left: **The East Camp in 1922.** By this time it was the home of the Boys Wing, Cadet College. The Boys Wing had been established at the end of the Great War and with the completion of the East Camp buildings the Air Council decided to use Cranwell as the base for No.1 School of Technical Training (Boys). Initially called the Boy Mechanics School and then the Boys Training Wing the name was changed to No.2 School of Technical Training (Boys) but in 1921 reverted to the title Boys Wing, Cadet College and later moved to Halton. In October 1925 it became No.4 (Apprentices) Wing and as such returned from RAF Halton in 1926.

Above left: **The Cranwell Light Aeroplane Club was formed by staff and pupils of the college in 1923 under the guidance of Flt Lt Nicholas Comper. The club's first aeroplane, the CLA 2 (the CLA 1 only reached the design stage) – competed in the 1924 Lympne Light Plane Trials and, flown by its designer, Flt Lt Comper, won the reliability trial. Encouraged by their success, the Club decided to enter the 1925 Trials with a new aircraft. Comper's design for the CLA 3 was for a single seat parasol monoplane seen here. Powered by a 32 hp Bristol Cherub engine the aircraft had a top speed of 100 mph and won the International Speed race. In 1926 the aircraft was entered in the King's Cup Air Race but had to force land due to engine trouble. It was scrapped in 1929.**

Top: **Aerial view of the south airfield taken in 1924. The Lighter Than Air Section had already gone but the original road leading to it, still in use today and now called Lighter Than Air Road, can be seen to the right of the picture. The F-type hangars are conspicuous in the foreground.**

Above right: **The CLA 4 was unusual in that it was a biplane with an inverted sesquiplane layout, the upper wing being shorter and narrower than the bottom wing. The club decided to build two CLA 4s and both were entered for the 1926 Lympne Trials. G-EBPB was completed with a Cherub engine and flew in the Trials but was eliminated with a damaged undercarriage. It did fly in various other events before being scrapped in 1933. The second aircraft, G-EBPC, was unable to compete in the trials because of a lack of engine; it crashed in March 1927.**

Top: **Armstrong Whitworth Siskin III J7174.**
The Siskin III shared with the Gloster Grebe
the distinction of being one of the first fighters
to be selected to re-equip the RAF's fighter
squadrons after the Great War, superseding
Sopwith Snipes from 1923. In the training role
a number were converted to dual control.
Siskins replaced the ageing Snipe at Cranwell
in 1927.

Centre left: **Avro 504K H3073 in a sorry state**
after a flying accident, 1926.

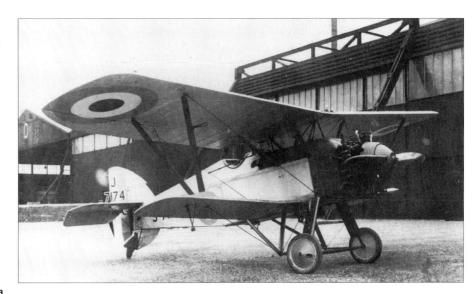

Centre right: **Cranwell, with its long runway,**
was used on a number of occasions for
development flying and as a starting point for a
number of record attempts. On 20th May 1927,
J8607, a modified Hawker Horsley torpedo
bomber, left the airfield on a flight that was to
last 34½ hours, ending when engine trouble
forced the aircraft down in the Persian Gulf.
The distance of 3,419 miles constituted a new
world record; to be broken within a few hours
by Charles Lindberg on his New York to Paris
flight. Two more attempts were made from
Cranwell with a second Horsley. On 6th June
1927 the aircraft was forced to land at
Martlesham Heath with engine problems. A
third and final attempt ended with a forced
landing in the River Danube.

Bottom: **The Gloster II, G-EBJZ, was the**
second aircraft built to contest the 1925
Schneider Trophy. The first aircraft sank and
was lost before pre-race trials. With the race
postponed until the following year 'BJZ had its
floats removed and a wheeled undercarriage
fitted. The aircraft was prepared as a testbed
for equipment to be used in a new seaplane
racer. Cranwell was one of the few airfields
that had sufficient runway length to enable the
aircraft to be tested safely. Unfortunately, on
11th June 1925 when undertaking a high speed
run at about 40 ft over the airfield, the aircraft
developed problems and crashed. Larry Carter
Gloster's Chief Test Pilot, was seriously
injured and died on 27th September 1925.

Hinchliffe's laatste tocht .... en ondergang!

Hinchliffe, de bloemige vliegheld, dien we hier uit de dagen der "Elta" en uit de eerste jaren der K.L.M. nog zoo kenden, is gebleven als offer van den Oceaan. 't Mag gezegd dat zijn tocht al een zeekheen was als de van veler anderen; zonder deugelijke hulp, alleen met een 25-jarige jonge vrouw die een groot vliegen zocht, maar als heldendochter he naar serenitynen .... Hierboven in het vliegtuig "Federman", waarmee de tragische tocht ondernomen werd, bij 't veel gebeide, daarnaar Miss Mackay en Hinchliffe en rechts .... de mest tragische figuren uit dit drama : zij, die overleden Mevrouw Hinchliffe, naar men weet een Hollandsche — als Tazberg — van geboorte, en haar twee jonge kinderen !

Above: **One of the station's former wartime instructors, Captain W G R Hinchcliffe, returned to Cranwell at the end of February 1928 with Endeavour, his Stinson SM-1 Detroiter mono-plane X4183 (not 41831 as painted on the aircraft), serial no.223, to prepare for an east-west crossing of the Atlantic Ocean. Hinchcliffe took off at 08.35am on 13th March, and was last seen heading into the Atlantic from the coast of Ireland. Nothing more was ever heard of him or his passenger, the heiress Elsie Mackay. His disappearance caused consider-able speculation at the time, especially in Holland, where his wife and family remained.** John Underwood collection, via Chris Salter

Top right: **Cranwell again became the scene for a long distance record attempt on 24th April 1929. The purpose-built Fairey Long Range Monoplane J9479 took off from a specially prepared runway, made of rolled ash, for its first attack on the record. Fifty hours and 4,130 miles later the flight ended at Karachi due to bad weather and fuel shortage. This set a new England-India record but did not achieve a world distance record.** via J D Oughton

Opposite page centre: **Fairey Long Range Monoplane J9479 returns to Cranwell in triumph after its record breaking England to India flight.**

Opposite page bottom: **Sqn Ldr A.G.Jones-Williams and Flt Lt N.H.Jenkins, the crew of the Fairey Long Range photographed in front of their aircraft shortly before the second attempt on the distance record. The flight, starting on 16th December 1929, was routed towards** Capetown but, tragically, after 13½ hours the aircraft encountered turbulence over North Africa and crashed into the foothills of the Atlas Mountains with the loss of both crew members.

Right: **The Sopwith Cuckoo, one of the earliest landplane torpedo bombers, pictured on a visit to the station in 1922. N6923 was at that time being operated by 210 Squadron.**

Above: **DH 9a J7089 is not recorded as being on strength at Cranwell and was probably visiting when this photograph was taken about 1925, note the suitcase on the wing. It had been converted to dual control at Kenley and then saw service with 24 and 39 Squadrons.**

Centre right: **Just visiting! The DH 10 was one of the RAF's promising new bombers, unfortunately arriving too late to see action in the Great War. Post war its main use was as a mail carrier, chiefly in the Middle East. Only one unit, 120 Squadron, was equipped with the type in Britain and it is probably from that unit that this example, seen festooned with cadets, comes. The picture is dated 1922.**

Right: **A visitor to Cranwell in 1925 was Blackburn Dart N9999. The Dart was designed as a torpedo carrier for the Fleet Air Arm, one of the early designs in a long association that the Blackburn Company had with torpedo dropping aircraft. The Dart appeared in 1921 and 117 aircraft were built before production ceased in 1927, with the aircraft not being declared redundant until 1935.**

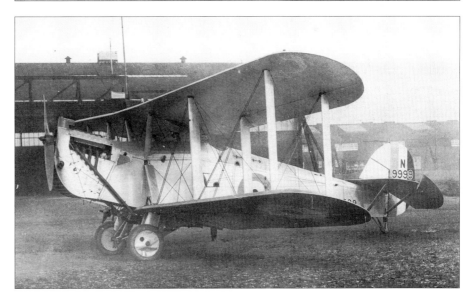

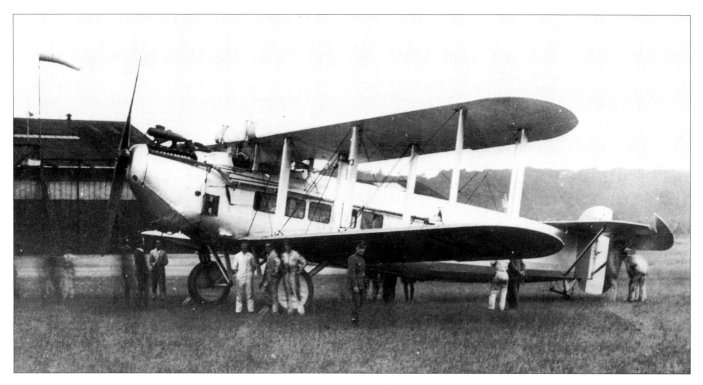

Above: **Our final selection of aircraft visiting Cranwell in the 1920s, begins with this rarity – an Avro 561 Andover. Only three of these aircraft (J7261-J7263), a transport version of the Aldershot bomber, were supplied for service with the RAF. The type was also used for ambulance trials and with a capacity of twelve passengers was also leased for trials with Imperial Airways.**

Left: **Probably the first amphibian to land at Cranwell, this Supermarine Seamew N212 paid a visit during 1928. 'We put out the anchor when finishing our taxying run', so said the caption!**

Left: **26th April 1929. The foundation stone for a new college building is laid by Lady Maude Hoare, wife of the Secretary of State for Air, Sir Samuel Hoare.**

Below left: **By July 1931 work on the new college building was progressing apace. The mighty steel structure, designed to carry the weight of the dome, is seen here being assembled.**

Below right: **By late 1932 most of the external work had been completed on the new college hall, although scaffolding surrounds the tower.**

Top left: **The official opening ceremony of the new college hall took place on 11th October 1934 and was performed by HRH The Prince of Wales, later King Edward VIII.**

Top right: **With the opening of the new college building and the provision of new student accommodation, the quality of cadet life improved.**

Bottom: **When the Armstrong Whitworth Atlas began to enter squadron service in 1927, it became the first type to have been designed from the outset as an army co-operation aircraft, superseding the veteran Bristol Fighter in that role. Production of the Atlas continued until 1933 and of the 449 aircraft constructed, 146 were built with dual controls and were supplied to the RAF as advanced trainers. Atlas Trainers began to replace the DH9A at Cranwell in 1930.**

Top: **During the inter war years flying accidents were a fairly common occurrence, a typical example is this Armstrong Whitworth Atlas Trainer, K1186, which crashed in October 1930. The pilot, Flight Cadet E H Fawkes, was killed.**

Above: **Continuing the tradition of Avro trainers in the RAF, the Avro Tutor was chosen to replace the Avro 504N in 1932. In 1933 it superseded the 'N' at Cranwell and went on to become the standard elementary trainer with the RAF until replaced in 1939. Note the 'quartered' wheels, typical of many Cranwell aircraft.**

Above: **The Hawker Fury I single seat fighter member of the pre-war Hawker family of successful bi-plane aircraft was also operated at Cranwell in the mid-1930s. K5678 served at No.3 FTS before arriving at Cranwell (note the College Arms on the fin). In September 1940 this particular aircraft was transferred to the South African Air Force.**

Below: **The Hawker Hart appeared at Cranwell in 1934. This most adaptable aircraft was designed as a day bomber and entered squadron service in 1930. A number of Harts were completed as dual control trainers and both versions saw service with the college. In our photograph, K3844 in the foreground, is a standard machine while those in the background have dual controls.**

Above: **K2345 was built as a Vickers Victoria Mk.V but in January 1935 was converted to a Valencia and posted to the E&W School. This particular machine ended its days in an overshoot at Catterick on 4th September 1939.**

Above and left: **In November 1937, two De Havilland 86B airliners were delivered to the E&W School. L8037 and L8040 had been constructed in May 1936 and registered to British Airways as G-ADYC and 'DYD respectively. After service at Cranwell both aircraft were transferred to 24 Squadron and then later on to the Admiralty.** MAP

HERES GEORGE

"George"

WE welcome back F/Sgt. Anderson to the Instrument Makers' School, from the R.A.F. Station at Mildenhall, where he was for some time in charge of the Automatic Control Station.

F/Sgt. Anderson is one of the very few ex-Royal Flying Corps Instrument Makers still in the Service and his association with the E. & W. School extends over some 20 years. He is still greatly interested in the sporting activities of the School, and particularly in those of " C " Squadron, to whose personnel he is engaged also in disclosing the mysteries of his trade.

The photograph illustrates " George," the demonstration Automatic Control Set as arranged for the visit of His Majesty the King to Mildenhall, when F/Sgt. Anderson and two ex-apprentices had the honour of demonstrating it.

C. B. T.

Above: **This aerial view of Cranwell's 1937 Empire Air Day demonstrates the informality of the occasion with the lack of crowd barriers and the public mingling with the aircraft. This photo shows aircraft on the South airfield with buildings of East Camp in the background.**

Below: **In October 1937 Cranwell played host to a group of German Luftwaffe officers led by General Erhard Milch, chief of Luftwaffe Air Staff, then on an official visit to Britain. In the background are the two De Havilland 86 airliners that were used by the visiting Germans; one (L7596) a 24 Squadron aircraft while the other (owned by Blackpool and West Coast Air Services Ltd) carries the civil registration G-AENR.**

Opposite page, top left: **The Electrical and Wireless School arrived at Cranwell in September 1929 and was resident on the station, under various titles, until 1952. During that time the unit operated a wide variety of aircraft. This De Havilland 60M Moth K1830 was on strength during the mid-1930s.**

Opposite page, bottom left and right: **Reproduced from the December 1937 edition of The E&W School magazine, this extract gives the origins of the nick-name 'George', commonly used during the Second World War in connection with the automatic pilot.**

The 1930s

Above: **Cadets watch an instructor attaching 20lb Cooper bombs to the underwing racks of Hawker Audax K4391. The Cooper bomb had appeared in 1917 and was still in use up to the outbreak of World War II. Audax K4391 eventually crashed attempting a forced landing near Stony Stratford, Buckinghamshire, on the 9th December 1939.**

Left: Instructor and pupil prepare for a night training flight in Hawker Hart Trainer K3754. Following the Munich crisis of 1938 training aircraft lost their overall silver finish and took on a more warlike look with upper surfaces painted in green and brown camouflage finish, and yellow lower and under surfaces.

Bottom: **Trainee pilots prepare a route in front of their Airspeed Oxford aircraft, in what is probably a posed photograph, one of a series taken to welcome the Oxford to Cranwell in 1938. The Airspeed Oxford was the first twin-engined monoplane advanced trainer to enter service with the RAF at the end of 1937. The 'Ox-box' as it was known, had a distinguished career, serving at Cranwell until the end of 1950. The type was finally withdrawn from RAF training with the closure of No.10 AFTS Pershore, in 1954.**

Below and right: **At a 1939 open day, engineering students demonstrate patching instruction, using the hull of Supermarine Southampton M638, one of many retired air-frames used at Cranwell for instructional purposes.**

THE 1940s

Below: **The Miles Master was developed from a private venture design for a high speed monoplane trainer, the Miles Kestrel. The Master I began to be introduced into service in May 1939 fitted with a Rolls Royce Kestrel engine, followed in November 1939 by the Mk.II powered by a Bristol Mercury radial engine. The final version, the Master III pictured here, was fitted with a Pratt and Whitney Wasp Junior engine and first flew in 1940. The Master was used in quantity at Cranwell throughout the war years.**

Left: **The first-ever jet-propelled flight in Britain was made from Cranwell's runway on the evening of 15th May 1941. The little Gloster E28/39, powered by a single Whittle W-1 turbojet engine of only 860lb thrust, took off at 7.15pm for a flight that lasted 17 minutes. Fifteen more flights, with a total of 10 hours flying time, were completed before the aircraft left the airfield at the end of the month.**

Right: **Despite several German air raids on the airfield, the College Hall escaped damage from enemy action. The only serious war-time damage came on the night of 19th March 1942 when A.W. Whitley P5052 of Cranwell-based No.3 (Coastal) OTU crashed onto the roof of the building during a night exercise, killing the 3-man crew and injuring three airmen in the college. The ensuing fire seriously damaged the west end of the building. Temporary repairs were carried out with more permanent rebuilding not being undertaken until 1946.**

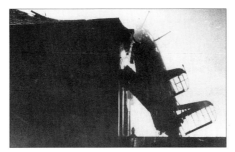

Above: **Next morning the extent of the damage caused by Whitley P5052 was evident.**

Centre right: **The first post-war royal visit took place on 13th June 1945 when King George VI inspected members of No.19 FTS who still occupied the college building, the college proper not re-opening until October 1946.**

Bottom right: **The North American Harvard was one of the first American types to enter service with the RAF when the first aircraft were delivered to RAF Spitalgate in December 1938. The first Harvards arrived at Cranwell in September 1944 to join the strength of 19 FTS. When 19 FTS departed from the station in April 1947, Harvards remained at Cranwell to form 'A' Flight of the re-opened college's flying wing. When the flying wing was re-organised into two squadrons in September 1948, No.2 Squadron comprised three flights of Harvards, with the type remaining in service at Cranwell until 1954. Harvard II FT302, coded GJ of 19 FTS was photographed in November 1945, whilst formating with another of the same type.**

Top left: **Main variant of the Harvard used by Flying Training Command post-war was the IIB. 'AN' of Cranwell's 19 FTS, was photographed in 1946, still in the all-yellow scheme. A four-letter code system (for training aircraft plus those of RAF Reserve Command) was introduced that same year, and used until 1951.** *RAF Museum P7404 via Bill Taylor.*

Top right: **The Percival Prentice superseded the veteran Tiger Moth as the RAF's basic trainer late in 1947. In July 1948 it was introduced into service at Cranwell and equipped the two flights of 'A' Squadron of the flying school. This photograph of VS284 is dated 1948.** *R Sturtivant.*

Bottom: **As early as 1941, Avro Ansons were used at Cranwell by No.3 (Coastal) Operational Training Unit. In April 1947, when the RAF College was officially reformed as an independent unit, instead of a combined College/FTS, the flying wing was reorganised into three flights, one of which ('C' Flight) was equipped with Ansons for navigational training. The post war four-letter coding is again visible, 'FA' was allocated to 19 FTS from 1946 to 1947 thereafter it denoted RAF College until 1951. 'GA' are the individual aircraft code letters.** *R Sturtivant.*

With the threat of imminent invasion, airfields began to develop defence systems to combat possible ground and air attack. This high level aerial photograph of Cranwell, allegedly dated 13th June 1940, has been overmarked with the positions of the various measures taken to defend the airfield. What appear to be several Airspeed Horsa assault gliders parked outside the North airfield centre hangars, raises a doubt as to the correct date of the photograph.

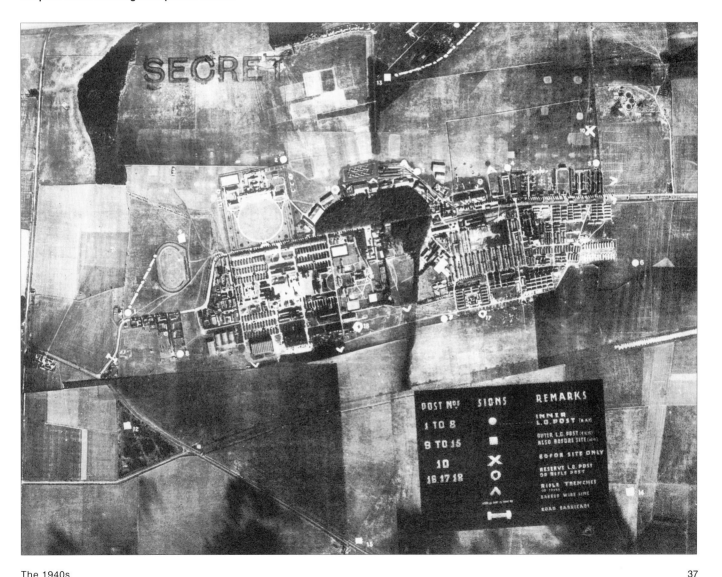

THE 1950s

Top left and right: **Installing the peal of bells presented to the College in 1952 by the Shell Petroleum Company. Each evening, when the ensign is lowered, the bells ring 'retreat' as a daily reminder of those 477 cadets who lost their lives during the Second World War. The Shell plaque is situated in the foyer to College Hall.**

Above: **Group Captain H J Wilson in front of the Gloster Meteor IV record breaker EE549, on 10th June 1952, shortly after its arrival at Cranwell. He had previously established a new world air speed record of 606mph in EE454, another Meteor IV, on 7th November 1945. EE549 was one of many airframes that formed a Museum at Cranwell around this period. Some of these later found their way into store at nearby RAF Fulbeck and fortunately survived to become exhibits in various museums today. EE549 was one of those that survived and following numerous moves over the years (St Athan, Hendon, Abingdon, St Athan, Cosford) is currently on display in the Tangmere Military Aviation Museum, West Sussex.**

Photographs on the opposite page:

Top left: **The de Havilland Company's own successor to its venerable Tiger Moth was the Chipmunk. Designed by the Company's Canadian Division it first flew in Toronto in May 1946. Adopted as an** ab initio **trainer by the RAF, the Chipmunk T.10 replaced the Prentice at Cranwell in 1952 and remained in service until superseded by the piston Provost in 1954, although some remained on strength long after that date. In this 1968 photograph of WG308, day-glo striping has replaced the yellow 'T' (trainer) bands applied to training aircraft in the late 1950s; also note the light blue fuselage band, with dark blue edging that has become a feature of RAF College aircraft. Basic fuselage colour is the light aircraft polyurethane grey; with serials and codes in black. MAP**

Top right: **A short-lived advanced trainer, the Boulton Paul Balliol T.2, appeared at Cranwell in 1954. Powered by a Rolls Royce Merlin engine the Balliol had formed the equipment of only one other unit, No.7 FTS at RAF Cottesmore. Within two years of arriving at Cranwell it had been completely replaced by the Vampire T.11 jet trainer. MAP**

Bottom: **After the Anson had ended its service in the training role, this ubiquitous type soldiered on as a communication transport for at least a further 10 years. C.19 VM312 was one such 'hack', and is seen here in 1957. Note again the Cranwell 'band' around the rear fuselage. MAP**

Top left and centre: **The Hunting-Percival Provost T.1 was adopted as the standard basic trainer for the RAF in 1953, when it replaced the Prentice. The De Havilland Vampire T.11, a two seat trainer version of the famous Vampire fighter, had been introduced into service in 1952. When the two types arrived at Cranwell in 1954 a new scheme of pilot training was introduced. This was referred to as the Provost/Vampire sequence. Our photographs show Provost T.1 XF893 coded JP, taken in 1958 and Vampire T.11 XE936 coded 51.** Photographs courtesy MAP.

Bottom left: **Single seat Vampire FB.5s and FB.9s, on becoming obsolete with first-line squadrons of the RAF, were employed at a number of training establishments, including Cranwell, to provide single seat experience as a follow on to the Provost/Vampire T.11 syllabus. At some FTSs they were used as an operational trainer in ground attack and rocket-firing techniques. These late production FB.9s of the College, coded 9, 5, 21 and 14, are WX226, WX204, WR242 and WR247 respectively.**

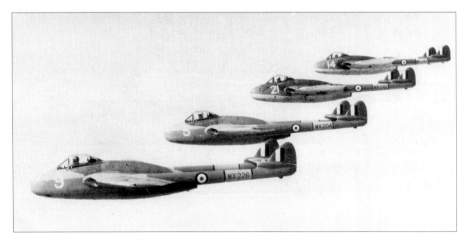

Above: **Another RAF College Vampire FB.9. Here, WP991 coded 38, unfortunately undated, displays a variation in colour scheme: the fuselage appears to be in an all silver finish compared to the camouflaged scheme evident on the examples in the adjacent photograph and on the front cover.** R C B Ashworth via W J Taylor.

Above: **A trio of Cranwell based Provost T.1s fly in formation past College Hall in November 1954. They are, individually: WW425, WW394, and WW423, coded DS, DD and DM respectively.** W J Taylor collection.

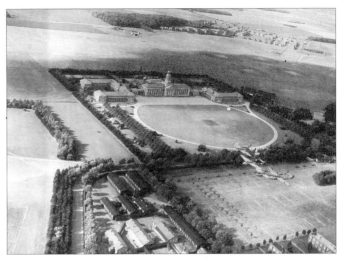

Above: **This photograph, taken on 27th June 1957, was almost certainly staged on the same occasion as our front cover photograph. It shows four RAF College Vampire FB(T).9s, WX221 '4', WX215 '12', WR264 '29', and WX225 '8', formating over College Hall and grounds. In the top right background are the married quarters, built on the site of the former Lighter Than Air Section site.** Flight 34978s.

Below: **The Vickers Valetta T.3 was a development of the Valetta C.1 transport aircraft, the military version of the Viking civil airliner. The T.3 'flying classroom' was designed for navigator training and entered service at Cranwell in 1955, when a flight of Valettas was added to the strength of the college.** MAP

Below: **Constructed as a replacement for the Vickers Wellington T.10 crew trainer, the Vickers Varsity entered RAF service with No.201 Advanced Flying School at RAF Swinderby in June 1951. In 1957 Varsities joined the Valettas at Cranwell, eventually replacing them in the navigator training role. Varsities remained in use until 1972 when navigator training at Cranwell was phased out .** MAP

Above: **Her Majesty Queen Elizabeth II naming Queens Avenue at Cranwell in 1960.**

Right: **An aerial view of Trenchard Hall taken around the time of its completion in mid 1966.**

Below: **Sir Frank Whittle, originally a boy entrant to the Cadet College and, of course, inventor of the jet engine, returned to Cranwell on 4th October 1962 to name the new instructional building 'Whittle Hall', after himself.**

Below: **On 17th May 1966 the Rt Hon Viscount Trenchard of Wolfeton, the only surviving son of the first Viscount Trenchard, Chief of Air Staff 1919-1929, named the new Department of Engineering building 'Trenchard Hall'.**

Above: **Flying training at Cranwell became all-jet in 1961 when the Jet Provost replaced both the piston Provost and the Chipmunk in the basic training role. Pupil pilots were now able to receive the whole of their training on jet types. Initially, T.3 and T.4 variants equipped the School. Three T.3s, XN496 '31', XN495 '34' and XM455 '16', are seen here in the very early silver scheme with day-glo orange areas on nose, tip-tanks and rear fuselage. Only '16' has had the College Coat of Arms superimposed on the white disc on its upper forward fuselage.**

Centre right: **This photograph, taken in 1968, shows Jet Provost T.4 XP559 '74' in the silver scheme with high visibility day-glo red strips on the nose, tip tanks and rear fuselage. In the early 1970s the T.4s were replaced by the improved and pressurised T.5s .** MAP.

Top right: **For many years the RAF College Glider Flight has operated a number of craft, usually from the North airfield site. Types used by the Flight, which provided Air Experience for Officer Cadets of the RAF College, have included Kirby Cadets, Slingsby Prefects and Sedberghs. They have normally worn full college markings, such as on this Sedbergh TX.1 WG498, photographed in October 1975.** MAP

Right: **Hawker Siddeley HS.125 Dominies of the former RAF College of Air Warfare at Manby moved to Cranwell in January 1974 when the CAW became the Department of Air Warfare of the RAF College. They wore a stylised version of the Cranwell blue band, as seen on XS733 in March 1976. In early 1978 the Dominies were passed to 6 FTS at Finningley, Yorkshire.** MAP

When the Engineering Officer training function was transferred from Henlow to Cranwell in 1966, the Servicing Instruction Flight was set up in a solitary T2 hangar, near to the Aerodynamic and Thermodynamic Laboratory site on the extreme eastern edge of Cranwell South airfield. The flight was issued with a variety of retired aircraft which were used to give student engineering officers practical experience of aviation servicing in an operational environment. To meet the requirements of this unit, the aircraft were maintained in a taxiable condition. In more recent years these aircraft have been replaced by several Hunters and examples of the Jet Provost, Harrier and Jaguar.

Vulcan B.1 XA901/7897M arrived in November 1965, and was eventually broken up on site in September 1972. Lightning F.1 XG329/8050M, was at Cranwell by May 1970 and when eventually surplus to requirements, found its way to the fire compound at RAF Swinderby. Canberra B(I)8 WT339/8198M arrived 27th June 1972 and when withdrawn ended its days on the fire dump at Barkston Heath. Sea Vixen FAW.2 XJ609/8172M was taken on strength at Cranwell in September 1971 and departed to Abingdon on 14th November 1980. The latter three were all photographed in January 1975.
All W J Taylor

The 1980s and 1990s

Top left: **In the early 1970s, the Jet Provost T.4s were replaced by the pressurised T.5. The flying training element of the RAF College became known as the Basic Flying Training School and by early 1980 had standardised its fleet on the Jet Provost T.5A, a later variant of the Mk.5, identifiable by the handle-shaped glide slope aerial, on the nose. This example, XW334 '39', was photographed at its home base in 1980.** MAP.

Centre left: **Several Bulldog T.1 primary training aircraft have been in use at Cranwell in the last few years. This example, photographed in July 1993, is believed to be one of the half dozen or so operated by the Royal Air Force College Air Squadron. This unit provides air experience flying for the cadets of the Department of Initial Officer Training. XX700, coded 'B1', has the blue fuselage band, blue/white/red vertical stripes on the tailplane, and in a nice flashback to the 1930s – quartered wheels.** MAP

Below: **In 1991 No.3 Flying Training School at Cranwell began to phase out the Jet Provost in favour of the Shorts Tucano T.1 – a marque developed from the Brazilian Embraer Tucano – and by April 1993 had 59 of the type on strength. ZF295 was seen at the 'Battle of Britain' Air Show at Finningley on 19th September 1992. The tradition of the light blue/dark blue 'Cranwell' fuselage band continues to this day.** MAP.

RAF COLLEGE FLYING CLUB

Right: **Over the years, the RAF College Flying Club has operated a number of Tiger Moths, of which G-ANEF was the longest serving. It is seen here at Cranwell on 31st March 1974, undergoing Certificate of Airworthiness renewal. It was later repainted in its former military colours as T5493, but was damaged beyond economical repair in an accident on 17th September 1988. It is now in Sweden where it is being rebuilt to flying condition.** W J Taylor.

Centre left: **Robin Aiglon G-CRAN, together with stablemate Robin Alpha G-RAFC, were operated by the Flying Club from 1980, until replaced by a pair of Grob G-115As, G-RAFA and G-RAFB in 1989. G-CRAN was photographed at Cranwell in 1980. Could the diagonal stripe on the tail be another variation of the traditional Cranwell blue band?** MAP.

Left: **Grob 115A G-RAFA is seen at Spanhoe, on 24th April 1993.** John Smith.

UNITS THAT HAVE BEEN
BASED AT CRANWELL

Unit	Dates		Representative Aircraft Types
RNAS Central Training Establishment (HMS *Daedalus*)	4.16 to	3.18	BE2, Avro 504, Camel, Balloons, Airships
Electrical & Wireless School	5.16 to	6.18	Various
Airship Training Wing	4.18 to	.19	Balloons, Airships
201 Training Depot Station	.18 to	7.18	Camel
202 Training Depot Station	.18 to	7.18	BE2c, DH9
213 Training Depot Station	6.18 to	7.18	Avro 504K
HQ 12 Group	.18 to	.18	-
56 Training Depot Station	7.18 to	2.20	BE2, Avro 504, Camel, Pup
57 Training Depot Station	7.18 to	2.20	BE2, Avro 504, Camel
58 Training Depot Station	7.18 to	.19	Avro 504K, 0/400
Boys Training Wing	.18 to	3.20	-
Wing Aeroplane Repair Section	.18 to	.19	-
Royal Air Force Cadet College	5.2.20 to	1.29	DH9A, Avro 504K, Bristol Fighter, Snipe, Siskin
School of Technical Training (Boys)	3.20 to	1.5.21	Various airframes
Boys Wing, Cadet College	5.21 to	10.25	Various airframes
RAF Hospital	.22 to	.40	-
No.4 (Apprentices) Wing	10.25 to	1.1.36	Various airframes
Royal Air Force College	1.29 to	3.8.39	Bristol Fighter, Atlas, Fox, Tutor, Hart, Avro 504K, Avro 504N, Bulldog, Audax, Fury, Hector, Oxford
1 Electrical & Wireless School	8.29 to	9.40	Wallace, Valencia
School of Store Accounting and Store Keeping	7.34 to	12.36	-
Equipment Training School	12.36 to	6.41	-
Supplies Depot	10.36 to	11.49	-
School of Clerks Accounting	.39 to	.41	-
Royal Air Force College Service Flying Training School	3.8.39 to	20.3.44	Oxford, Blenheim, Master
HQ 21 Group	12.39 to	7.44	-
2 Flying Instructors School	10.9.40 to	11.40	Tutor, Oxford
1 Signals School	9.40 to	1.41	Wallace, Anson, Oxford
2 Central Flying School	11.40 to	6.41	Tutor, Oxford
1 Radio School	3.41 to	1.43	Proctor, Dominie
3 (Coastal) Operational Training Unit	6.8.41 to	23.1.43	Anson, Whitley, Wellington, Lysander
8 Radio School	1.43 to	6.46	Proctor, Dominie, Halifax, Harvard
17 Service Flying Training School	20.3.44 to	1.5.45	Oxford, Blenheim, Master, Spitfire, Harvard
19 Flying Training School	1.5.45 to	12.4.47	Tiger Moth, Anson, Oxford, Harvard
Royal Air Force College	18.4.42 to date		Tiger Moth, Prentice, Harvard, Chipmunk, Provost, Anson, Vampire, Meteor, Jet Provost, Valetta, Varsity, (HS) Dominie.

Unit	Dates	Representative Aircraft Types
6 Radio School	10.50 to 12.50	Oxford
3 Initial Training Squadron	1.51 to 3.53	Chipmunk
Servicing Instruction Flight	1.66 to date	Various aircraft
Department of Air Warfare	1.74 to 30.6.93	(HS) Dominie to 9.77
Department of Specialist Ground Training	1.74 to date	Various aircraft (as at S.I.F.)
Central Flying School	12.4.76 to 9.77	Jet Provost
Basic Flying Training School	7.8.79 to 1.2.89	Jet Provost
Department of Initial Officer Training	4.80 to date	-
3 Flying Training School	1.2.89 to date	Jet Provost, Tucano
HQ University Air Squadrons	? to date	(Bulldog)
Directorate of Recruiting and Selection (RAF)	31.8.92 to date	-
Royal Air Force College Air Squadron	1.93 to date	Bulldog

Below: **The Cranwell Aviation Heritage Centre opened on 8th June 1992 to illustrate the history of Cranwell Air Station. It is situated about one mile South East of the airfield at Heath Farm, Rauceby. It is operated by North Kesteven District Council and opens daily 9am-5pm except Christmas Day and New Year's Day.** P H T Green.

Below: **The official opening ceremony was performed by Air Vice-Marshal David Cousins, the then Commandant of the College, seen here with Councillor Ewan A Robertson, Chairman of North Kesteven District Council. To the right is Mr Tony Ireland of Ireland Farms Ltd, owners of Heath Farm.** P H T Green.

Back cover illustrations: **This trio of Cranwell-based aircraft illustrate some of the changes in training aircraft colour schemes that have occurred over the past thirty years or so. Tucano T.1 ZF212 was photographed at Cranwell on 18th September 1991** (John Hale);

the Jet Provost T.4 XP583 attended the Gaydon 'Battle of Britain - At Home' on 15th September 1962, whilst the Chipmunk T.10 WG301 was present at a Lincolnshire Aero Club Fly-in at Hemswell in May 1969. Roy Bonser.